Pebble™

First Biographies

Jane Goodall

by Lola M. Schaefer and Wyatt Schaefer

Consulting Editor: Gail Saunders-Smith, PhD

Capstone
press

Mankato, Minnesota

Pebble Books are published by Capstone Press,
1710 Roe Crest Drive, North Mankato, Minnesota 56003.
www.capstonepress.com

Printed in China by Nordica.
0213/CA21300181
022013   007172R

Library of Congress Cataloging-in-Publication Data
Schaefer, Lola M., 1950–
    Jane Goodall/by Lola M. Schaefer and Wyatt Schaefer.
    p. cm.—(First biographies)
    Includes bibliographical references and index.
    ISBN-13: 978-0-7368-2083-7 (hardcover)
    ISBN-10: 0-7368-2083-3 (hardcover)
    ISBN-13: 978-0-7368-5085-8 (softcover pbk.)
    ISBN-10: 0-7368-5085-6 (softcover pbk.)
    1. Goodall, Jane, 1934– —Juvenile literature. 2. Primatologists—England—
Biography—Juvenile literature. 3. Chimpanzees—Tanzania—Gombe Stream
National Park—Juvenile literature. [1. Goodall, Jane, 1934– 2. Zoologists.
3. Scientists. 4. Women—Biography.] I. Schaefer, Wyatt S., 1978– II. Title.
III. Series: First biographies (Mankato, Minn.)
QL31.G58S36 2005
591'.092—dc22   2003024947

Summary: Simple text and photographs present the life of Jane Goodall.

Note to Parents and Teachers

The First Biographies series supports national history standards for
units on people and culture. This book describes and illustrates the
life of Jane Goodall. The photographs support early readers in
understanding the text. This book also introduces early readers to
subject-specific vocabulary words, which are defined in the
Glossary. Early readers may need assistance to read some words
and to use the Table of Contents, Glossary, Read More, Internet
Sites, and Index/Word List sections of the book.

Table of Contents

Time Line

1934
born

Early Years

Jane Goodall is a scientist who studies animals. Jane was born in 1934 in London, England. Her parents gave her a toy chimpanzee named Jubilee.

◄ Jane with her toy chimpanzee, Jubilee

Time Line

1934
born

Jane liked to learn about animals. She read books and visited zoos. Jane wrote her thoughts in a journal.

Time Line

1934
born

1957
travels
to Africa

Jane finished school
in 1952. In 1957,
Jane went to Africa.

Time Line

1934
born

1957
travels
to Africa

Living in Africa

In Africa, Jane met a famous scientist, Dr. Louis Leakey. She worked for him studying chimpanzees in the wild.

Jane (left) with Dr. Leakey

Time Line

1934
born

1957
travels
to Africa

In 1960, Jane moved to the Gombe reserve in Africa. She watched chimpanzees to see how they lived. Jane was one of the first people to learn that chimps make and use tools.

Time Line

1934
born

1957
travels
to Africa

1965
earns PhD from
Cambridge University

In 1962, Jane went
to England to go to
Cambridge University.
She graduated in 1965.
Then Jane returned to Africa
to continue her research.

Time Line

1934
born

1957
travels
to Africa

1965
earns PhD from
Cambridge University

Helping Wildlife

Jane created the Jane Goodall Institute in 1977. The institute has a program for children called Roots and Shoots. The program helps people, animals, and the environment.

◀ Jane with children from Africa

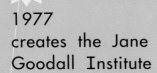

1977
creates the Jane
Goodall Institute

Time Line

1934
born

1957
travels
to Africa

1965
earns PhD from
Cambridge University

Jane has studied animals for about 40 years. She has written many books about her life. In 2002, Jane was named a United Nations Messenger of Peace.

◄ Jane with the leader of the United Nations in 2002

1977
creates the Jane
Goodall Institute

2002
serves as UN
Messenger of Peace

Time Line

| 1934 born | 1957 travels to Africa | 1965 earns PhD from Cambridge University |

Today, Jane speaks to people around the world. Jane shares her love of chimpanzees. She works for peace and the good treatment of all animals.

1977
creates the Jane
Goodall Institute

2002
serves as UN
Messenger of Peace

Glossary

chimpanzee—a large primate without a tail

environment—the natural world of land, water, and air

Gombe reserve—a protected area in western Africa where animals have space to live and food to eat

institute—a group that is set up to protect animals, people, and other causes

journal—a diary in which people regularly write down their thoughts and experiences

research—to study and learn about a subject

scientist—a person who studies science and the world

wild—an area that has been left in its natural state; people did not know how chimpanzees lived before Jane's research; chimpanzees had not been studied in the wild.

Read More

Goodall, Jane. *The Chimpanzees I Love: Saving Their World and Ours.* New York: Scholastic, 2001.

Rinaldo, Denise. *Jane Goodall: With a Discussion of Responsibility.* Values in Action. Boston: Learning Challenge, 2003.

Shores, Erika L. *Chimpanzees: Living in Communities.* The Wild World of Animals. Mankato, Minn.: Bridgestone Books, 2005.

Internet Sites

FactHound offers a safe, fun way to find Internet sites related to this book. All of the sites on FactHound have been researched by our staff.

Here's how:

1. Visit *www.facthound.com*
2. Type in this special code **0736820833** for age-appropriate sites. Or enter a search word related to this book for a more general search.
3. Click on the **Fetch It** button.

FactHound will fetch the best sites for you!

Index/Word List

Word Count: 210
Early-Intervention Level: 20

Editorial Credits
Sarah L. Schuette, editor; Heather Kindseth, series designer and illustrator; Enoch Peterson, book designer; Kelly Garvin, photo researcher; Karen Hieb, product planning editor

Photo Credits
Courtesy of the Jane Goodall Institute, 4, 6, 8, 14; David S. Holloway/Apix, cover, 20; Hugo Van Lawick, 12; Joan Travis, 10; Michael Neugebauer, 1, 16; United Nations Department of Public Information, 18

Pebble Books thanks the Jane Goodall Institute for reviewing this book and for providing photographs.